ONCE UPON A DREAM

Surrey Dreams

Edited By Jenni Harrison

First published in Great Britain in 2017 by:

 Young**Writers** Est. 1991

Young Writers
Coltsfoot Drive
Peterborough
PE2 9BF
Telephone: 01733 890066
Website: www.youngwriters.co.uk

FOREWORD

Welcome to 'Once Upon a Dream – Surrey Dreams'.

For our 'Once Upon A Dream' competition, we invited primary school pupils to delve within their deepest imaginations and create poetry inspired by dreams. They were not limited to the dreams they experience during their sleep, they were free to explore and describe their dreams and aspirations for the future, what could inspire a dream, and also the darker side of dreams... the nightmare!

The topic proved to be hugely popular, with children dreaming up the cleverest, craziest and, sometimes, creepiest of poems! The entries we received showcase the writing talent and inspired imaginations of today's budding young writers.

Congratulations to James Haycock, who has been selected as the best poet in this anthology, hopefully this is a dream come true! Also a big well done to everyone whose work is included within these pages, I hope seeing it published help you continue living your writing dreams!

Jenni Harrison

CONTENTS

Sion Astley (10)	70
Tessy Olliff (8)	71
Jack Garnham (9)	72
Callum Postins (9)	73
Noah Light	74
Lilia Bouhoune (9)	75
Kyle Neate (9)	76
Albanie Barrett (9)	77
Alan Jakub Kraczewski (7)	78
Elodie Jeans Trouabal-Weremczuk (8)	79
Jacob Ieuan Davies (8)	80
Abigail Garen Larsen (7)	81

St Cyprian's Greek Orthodox Primary Academy, Thornton Heath

Zaria Hinds (10)	82
Lamek Samson (7)	83
Deon Nunoo (11)	84
Isabelle Bradbury (9)	86
Daniel Cort (8)	87
Nastasia Tingle (11)	88
Ellie Todorova (7)	89
Ioanna Karanasiou (9)	90
Peggy Stack (8)	91
Tyler Price-Frankson (11)	92
Alyssa Ama Amponsah (8)	93
Yolanda-Jewel Michael (8)	94
Shayla-Skye Salmon (7)	95
Zemira Hinds (7)	96
Alex Todorov (11)	97
Shanai Thomas (8)	98
Teairra Blissett (11)	99
Shamai Holder (8)	100
Alana Shabazz (7)	101
Crystal-Anne Michael (10)	102
Avaie Henry (8)	103
Glynise Kobiah (8)	104
Megan Findlator (8)	105
Alicia Okonma (9)	106
Tiana Paige Tal (11)	107
Fega Omoma (8)	108

Ana-Maria Cornea (11)	109
Blessing Babalola (9)	110
Rihanna Malcolm-Moore (8)	111
Photios Yiannaki (11)	112
Jaydon Wesley (7)	113
Eli Julian Joseph Zoil (9)	114
Sienna Ellul (9)	115
Mohammad Zakaria (11)	116
Artemis Apostolopoulou (11)	117
Natalia Phillipou (9)	118
Nathan Gonzalez Gabino (9)	119
Kwabena Boakye (8)	120

St Martin's CE (A) Junior School, Epsom

Mina Janes (8)	121
Tasneem Islam (7)	122
Elaine Woodward (8)	123

THE POEMS

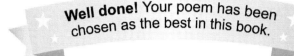

Dreaming Days

The other night I had a dream
I was lazing around, beside a stream
Calm blue water flowed gently by
And up above was a bright blue sky.

Colourful fish jumped here and there
And birdsong echoed through the air
The weeping willow shaded me
I paddled in water up to my knee.

The sparkling air was crisp and cool
And tadpoles flitted like glowing jewels
Dragonflies darted all around
While toadstools grew on mossy ground.

There was vibrant green grass on either side
And in the sun, playful otters dried
Shy deer grazed in the speckled light
Sunrays pierced the trees, shining bright.

On the horizon, mountains towered
And all around me plants flowered
I knew it just could not be real
It was almost too perfect, I could feel.

James Haycock (10)
Rokeby School, Kingston Upon Thames

The Dreams

T he giant broke into my room,
'H ey, go Pikachu, I choose you!'
E cstatically Pikachu made the giant meet his doom.

D reams all around me, squares, triangles
R ound ones too.
E legant dreams and ones so close together they get tangled
A ngels flying around making stew,
M y dreams are unstoppable,
S o yours are too.

Wait, no more acrostic, this is ballistic like a squid,
Squirt! There was a squid and he had to bid
For his long-lost kid.
Spiders everywhere.
Argh! There's one in the candy giant's hair.
Oh no, Gizmo escaped.
Bacon was falling from the sky.
There's Darth Vader and he's nicely caped.
Snap! 'So it was a dream!'
I'm still a normal guy!

James Macfarlane (10)
Rokeby School, Kingston Upon Thames

Dreams

In my dream
I am in a room
I dreamt of cream
but now I'm with Doom.
He guides me around
and said he is a writer.
I never thought
he was that kind of blighter.
In the room
on a silver plate
is a book
that decides people's fate.
He says he gets bored
so he invites people round.
The last one he called
they made such a sound
that the neighbours came around
and gave them a pound.
He says he doesn't know his meaning,
he writes but gets no pleasure.
That reminded me of a poem I was reading at school.
My teacher says it's a treasure.
Picking bits of bark off this rotten stump gives me no
pleasure

and it's no use so why do I do it?
Everyone was tasked to decipher that phrase
and some of the answers were as strange as a lime!
My friend told me that you dream of the days
so maybe that was happening at this very time.
He said he didn't know what he was
and I couldn't see through a cloud of fog.
He could have been a frog!
At last he waved his hands
and with some parting words
I will find myself.
He sent me back to the real world
and the dream thought to be a nightmare turned into
a happy dream.

Hugo Cotton (10)
Rokeby School, Kingston Upon Thames

Future Me

I dream of being an actor
Because I love being on the stage
I could even win an Oscar
By playing characters twice my age.

I dream of being a fashion designer
I'd sketch a dress with fancy bows
I think I'd make a million
Because everyone needs clothes.

I dream of being a writer
So I could use my imagination
I would write a best-selling novel
And would cheer people up with my creation.

I dream of being a film director
So I could boss people around
I'd pick the cast and build the sets
And help with the lights, music and sound.

I dream of being an artist
And get paid a high salary
I would paint the world and all my friends
And see my work in the National Gallery.

I dream of being an architect
So I could design an amazing landmark
I could even build a wooden boat
As good as Noah's ark.

I dream of what I might become
What I could be - the future me
But I haven't got a crystal ball
So we'll have to wait and see.

Fin Perry (11)
Rokeby School, Kingston Upon Thames

Dream

Air pushed swiftly past my face
As I flew across the city
I barely recognised the place
It all looked very pretty.

Lights twinkled below
Like stars in the sky.
Their beauty they don't know
Unless up here they fly.

How could I have been so blind
To look around the place.
The danger I did not find
A building in front of my face.

Bang!
I awoke with a start.
It should be morning
So how come it's still dark?

My eyes slowly focus
To see a figure tall.
A red nose that squeaks,
This can't be real at all.

A clown, it just can't be.
I must still be dreaming.
But somewhere in the dark,
I hear somebody screaming.

'There, there,' says a voice,
And I awake inside my bed.
'Don't worry darling, go back to sleep,
It was all inside your head.'

Jack Thomas (11)
Rokeby School, Kingston Upon Thames

My Dream Poem

Suddenly, the toffee portal opened and the enemy trooped through,
The mass of them grew and grew.
I saw them coming
Like candyfloss dimming.

The ongoing sea of soldiers stretched out as far as the eye could see,
They were not going to flee.
My army of ninjas rushed into war,
Huge jelly shurikens were all the eye saw.
I aimed the Haribo cannon and fired it at them, *bang!*
Then I charged out with my last men.

I soared up into the air on my confetti jet pack.
I aimed my popping candy pistols and fired them,
While doing a triple backflip.
I loaded another ammunition clip.
The two opposing sides were merged,
My army, like a wave, surged.

My ninjas loaded their cola throwers,
I turned up the music high.
Then I leant and dabbed,
'Cause I'm the only awesome guy.
Swiftly they fired,
They will never get tired.

George Mecrate-Butcher (10)
Rokeby School, Kingston Upon Thames

Dream

My eyes close
like a curtain on a stage.
The sad colour of loneliness
makes me run away.

Tall, angular trees stand upon me
like a dark city street.
The dream has arrived
and the journey now begins.

My mind wanders randomly
as my legs drag me aimlessly.
The nature around me
sends chills through my body.
Tall scary figures
send chills through my body.

Frightened like a turtle
I hide in my shell
waiting for the heavens
to send me to Hell.

The fox returns home
in its dark hole of blackness.
Torchlights start flashing
and the devils come shrieking.

The darkness has faded
and the dream escapes.
The next adventure awaits
yet still the clock ticks.

Amir Farah (11)
Rokeby School, Kingston Upon Thames

The Dream

Tossing and turning,
For sleep I'm yearning,
1, 2, 3 thoughts are clouding me,
Snakes under the bed, I can't get them out of my head,
Wizards and lizards create head blizzards.

Then finally a dream is made,
All those bad thoughts suddenly fade.
I was strolling in the sun,
When suddenly I heard a gun.

31 gnomes were charging down the street,
Firing poisonous marshmallows with their feet.
Bang, bang, bang they shot faster and I ran,
The bunch of evilness was closing in on me,
How would I ever get free?

Covered all around me, I tried to brush them away,
It was no use, it was impossible, there was no way,
Just as I thought the worst, a beam of stardust,
I lay in my bed,
It was okay.

Ollie Houghton (11)
Rokeby School, Kingston Upon Thames

Luke's Nightmare Landscape

The bubble of confidence bursting
As the teacher congratulates another.
The fear of not being good enough,
My hands over the result I then cover.

I'm a tight-rope walker above a valley,
My legs shake, my chest aches, my hands are so
clammy,
My foot shakes as I place it on the fraying rope,
I can hardly catch my breath; will I choke?

Is anything there? Black is all around,
I have to gain attention; that is the answer.
The pressure builds, my fear is growing every second,
What is there? Who is there? Who can I beckon?

A new nightmare for this generation would come,
A tyrant, an extremist, a threat that hurts everyone.
Wherever we go we will face this nightmare,
What can we do? How can we prepare?

Luke Taor (10)
Rokeby School, Kingston Upon Thames

The Dream

What's that footstep following but never passing by?
I turned around but of course there was nothing there,
I wonder why
But then I turn around again,
Then it is standing in the darkness.
How can it be standing there? What is it?
I can only feel fright,
Quickly and hastily it grabs me,
Oh what should I do? Who will save me, who?
Am I all alone? Is this the end? What should I do?
Suddenly, something else appears slithering like a
snake,
Powerful arms grab me and carry me away like I am a
Flake.
Then it takes me away from the foul creature behind.
No, it leaves me to save another person.
Am I sane in the mind?
Finally it comes and then I wake up
Even though I never found out who they were, at least I
woke up.

Daniel Robertshaw (11)
Rokeby School, Kingston Upon Thames

My Angel

In the silent world of forgotten dreams,
An angel lies and waits for me.
On fluffy clouds of marshmallows,
He sings sweet songs to all below.

With soft golden hair you just cannot miss,
He lights up the night with magical bliss.
I long to return to my bed every night,
To my faithful dream that I cherish so tight.

New adventures we share in the sky,
We fight dragons or perhaps even chase butterflies.
We've ventured upon ruthless pirates on Skull Bay
And even swum with mermaids on bright sunny days.

Sadly the new morning closes in too soon
And I have to leave my wonderful room.
I cannot wait to return to my bed,
To dream with my angel who lives in my head.

Cristian Iesini (10)
Rokeby School, Kingston Upon Thames

My Favourite Meals

I love food, I love food,
It puts me in a really good mood,
I really do love food, I really do,
I'd even eat a dim sum stew!

In the morning I have Nutella
And after Nutella I become a jolly good fella,
Oh I really love tea with Nutella too
And after tea you feel like a better you.

Then I feel I need to have lunch
'Cause I really don't want a brunch,
When I have lunch I have chicken and chips
And when there is salt I wipe it with my lips.

It is time for dinner, oh yes it is,
I only have it with a drink with strong fizz,
On the round table there is rice in the middle,
To eat the last grains is sure a large fiddle.

Ibraheem Al Saraf (11)
Rokeby School, Kingston Upon Thames

My Dream

One night last week I had a dream
I owned a marvellous sweet-making machine.
It blurted out treats left and right
all different flavours night after night.
My belly got rounder, my cheeks grew and grew,
climbing the stairs was hard work too.

Each day after school I'd run straight up the stairs
and stuff my face with Haribo bears.
But at school I was sad I'd lost all my desire
for maths, games and English and even for choir.
I began to realise that perhaps sweets aren't the best,
they make you unhealthy and really quite stressed.
Now the moral of this story is clear to see,
a well-balanced diet is the way forward for me!

Charlie Benjamin Bates (11)
Rokeby School, Kingston Upon Thames

Once Upon A Dream

Sunrays permeate the turquoise water
As waves gently deposit coral on the shore.
Splash! As the water carries on its journey.
You are powerless to this huge body of water.
Noise is drowned out by the peace and beauty of
undersea life.
Cocooned in warm waters like a womb
As the midnight blues glide by effortlessly.
How does this beauty go unnoticed?
Cool, soothing draughts blow in your hair
As you drift away overwhelmed by the beauty.
You are in your element,
Only to be disturbed by a jellyfish aimlessly making his
way up.
You swim back relaxed and with a low hum in your ear.
Suddenly, you awake and realise it was only a dream.

Rahul De Silva
Rokeby School, Kingston Upon Thames

Comparing Dreams

Two little siblings lying in bed,
Who knows what will fit in their head?
Are they prepared for the night ahead?
Will they pass the terrible test?

One of them dreams about rabbits and unicorns,
As all of the animals dance on lush, green lawns.
Beauty and pleasure surround one,
But will the other still have lots of fun?

The other dreams of mares in the night
And that she is involved in a fight.
As soon as the horses begin the chase
She thinks, *how can I escape from this terrible place?*

As the morning rises all the dreams
Are shut in the BFG's case.

Felix Peerless (11)
Rokeby School, Kingston Upon Thames

Weird Nightmares

N othing seemed right as I looked at this misty surrounding

I noticed in the corner of my eye, a peculiar thing

G rasping all my remaining energy, I looked closer

H ow does it look? I thought quicker

T he closer I drew it gave me more goosebumps than ever

M any scary, frightening things suddenly showed in front of me forever

A nd the things were dead - like zombies and enraged dragons

R arely, even clowns with scary faces shaped like polygons

E ven that would scare people who do not know the meaning of fear

S uddenly, my head shot up and I couldn't hear.

Joshua Peh (11)
Rokeby School, Kingston Upon Thames

Dream

Light
Tick, tick, tick, tick
Waves rolling onto their back
Tick, tick, tick, tick
Grass swaying to the rhythm of the wind
Tick, tick, tick, tick
Light seeping through the leaf
Tick, tick, tick, tick
Fire... crackling.

Darkness
Fire roaring
Tock, tock, tock, tock
Darkness overcoming the forest
Tock, tock, tock, tock
Wind making fields quiver
Tock, tock, tock, tock
Waves crashing down on the sea
Tock, tock, tock, tock
Flash purple, blue, red, white, orange, yellow, green
Ring.

Luke Weir (11)
Rokeby School, Kingston Upon Thames

Dream

Alone in my bedroom, I dream each night
Of trophies, cup wins, amazing sights.
Walls covered in heroes around my bed,
Incredible images flow through my head.

I practise each day, free kicks, quick feet,
Imagining playing in the Brazilian heat,
Each match, a small step, always playing to win,
The feeling's amazing, such fire from within.

And now I've made it, I've reached the World Cup,
My dream has been realised, I don't want to wake up.
I'm here with my teammates, representing our country,
The pride and the passion, just how I dreamed it would
be.

Charlie Jones (11)
Rokeby School, Kingston Upon Thames

Dream

What is this world of mist?
Is it a whole new realm, or somewhere few know exist?
Then a sudden sensation of rising
And I soar up and up and up into this world, ever
surprising.

And then I realise
This is no new world; it is the sky,
I am as light as a feather
Floating, flying, swooping.

Then a sudden sensation of plummeting
And I tumble down and down and down
Plunging into vastness
Down to my doom!

I see the cars rush towards me
And the houses loom ever nearer
And then I stop... dead?
Not dead; just back in my soft, snug bed!

Frederick Harvey (10)
Rokeby School, Kingston Upon Thames

A Different World

The sun shone on the deep blue waters
The ocean was still
With the blinding reflection of the sun,
Shining from above
A figure from underneath the surface swam past as I
jumped in.

Like a diving bell sinking deeper, I kept pushing down,
The salty waters stinging me
And I could finally see the coral
Shining from the glittering seabed.

Animals swam past
Like birds in the sky.
The beautiful blue ocean became crowded with
animals,
Like the murky streets of a city,
But a different world.
I glided back to the surface
Escaping this different world.

Freddie Thompson (10)
Rokeby School, Kingston Upon Thames

The Forest In My Dream

Beyond the rolling hills
And across the trickling stream
Lies the forest in my dream.

The trees sway in unison
Like the boats at a port
The remaining little rodents scurry to their burrows
Like small children chasing pigeons.

The frost bites the trees
On the gnarled swaying branches
Winter is approaching.

At first it went unnoticed
Then it came down in sheets
Covering everything in a cold sparkle of white.

The forest was quiet
Nothing stirred, until the days grew longer
And the sun embraced everything in its glow.

Arun Gayner (10)
Rokeby School, Kingston Upon Thames

I Dreamt I Was A Pilot

A mazing views you can see soaring through the turquoise sky

E ven a small old jet will make my heart flutter high

R ain or shine I will always fly my imaginary plane

O ne day a jumbo jet, the next a small Red Arrow

P iloting passengers around the globe

L ooping the loop like an agile acrobat

A ustralia could be a destination, or even outer space

N ever would you be in danger with me behind the controls

E choing the flight path like an expert, never faltering

S oaring at thirty thousand feet, I am ecstatic.

Alexander Charles Mallett (10)
Rokeby School, Kingston Upon Thames

The Weird Dream

Once I had a very weird dream,
It was about a mountainous pile of vanilla cream.

Once I had a very weird dream,
It was about a deadly moonbeam.

Once I had a very weird dream,
It was about someone who climbed a church with a jet
stream.

Once I had a very weird dream,
It was about a teacher who always used the
slipstream.

Once I had a very weird dream,
It was about a man who could eat steam.

Once I had a very weird dream,
It was about loads of alligators in a stream.

Edward Cheeseman (10)
Rokeby School, Kingston Upon Thames

The Shadow

Who are you so feeble and grey?
Why do you always show your face every day?
Keep your distance, get away from me!
I come unarmed,
Why is it just you and me?

Don't approach, stay away!
Go back home.
Far away.
Please stop following me.
I don't know the way!
Come on, please, not today.

At dawn you're as big as a mountain!
And at noon you're as tiny as a speck.
It's all the same, as if it were a game.
You follow me round like a rope around my neck.

Patrick James Priest (11)
Rokeby School, Kingston Upon Thames

What A Strange Dream I Had

I woke up one day
And said to myself,
'What a strange dream.'
I was at a different school,
This was no ordinary school.

The teachers were called Mum and Dad,
I asked Pip, but he was too astonished.
I went in the room,
'Hi son,' said the teacher.
'I'm not your son,'
I said in disgust.

I walked out,
Pip stood mesmerised,
Then I woke up.

Rory Crawshaw (10)
Rokeby School, Kingston Upon Thames

My Dream

When I snuggle up in bed
Dreams start whirring in my head.
My bed is like a rocket ship
Ready for another trip.
Where am I going tonight?
Will my dream be dark or light?
In my rocket ship I fly,
I leave my day behind, 'Bye-bye.'
I love the feeling of my dreaming
But sometimes I wake up screaming.
If I wake up with no fears
I say to God, 'Cheers.'

Oscar James (11)
Rokeby School, Kingston Upon Thames

Superpower Dream

U nder and over the small flapping birds

N iftily, he soars through the atmosphere

I nside, his heart is racing

C ourageously, attacking the wind

O utstandingly elegant

R acing through the sky

N ever to be stopped.

Daniel Singer (10)
Rokeby School, Kingston Upon Thames

The Dragon, The Knights And Me

One day it was blasting down with rain
Fffff and all the knights went insane
The dragons in their cave roaring
Then all of a sudden snoring.

The knights were only doing it for treasure
The treasure was as hard as gingerbread
But remember never wake the dragon up, never
But that dragon woke up and lost a feather.

All night the knights fight
The dragon was roaring
Every night it was a fright
The dragon was still roaring but the knights were
ignoring.

It was frightful outside
The dragon by my side
Everyone was trying to hide
But I had to tell them I lied.

Dragon, dragon, don't run away, please
I will give you the keys
I'm begging on my knees
And besides, I like your sneeze.

Your skin is as blue as the lovely sky
I will stop sighing
I know I shouldn't lie
And you're good at flying.

There you are
I didn't mean to make you fly so far
I will go in the car
Can I look in the money jar?

They might have found the treasure as gold as the sun
It is wonderful treasure
Phew, they have only found a feather
I'm glad they haven't found it yet
I have my time set.

The knights are here
I hope they aren't going to be in fear
It certainly doesn't smell good in here
Please say we're near.

We are here, we are here
And it is very, very clear
Thank goodness they haven't found the lovely treasure
yet
It's time to measure.

The star is shining bright
Hey, I've got a good sight
Anyway, I met a clever clown, it was freaky
Now we meet an owl.

What is going on?
Hey, that's our treasure
Anyway, I've got the key
Now I need that back.

The sky is pitch-black
Hooray, I've got the treasure back
Everything is a nightmare, it won't stop.

Never mind, keep running
In the huts bats wake, flying everywhere
Go back home
Home will be better
Tomorrow will be better.

The knights asked if they could meet me somewhere
So I said, 'Yes, sure, anywhere
Shall we become friends?
I won't forget to feed the hens.'

Rubi-Mae Ellis (9)
Springfield Primary School, Sunbury-On-Thames

Dream Planets

I fall through the carpet into nothingness,
Bump! A floor as cold as ice,
Where am I? Oh dear,
I have never seen this before, it's not nice.

Then, as fast as a lightning bolt,
I hurtle downwards, what is my head thinking?
Now, what's this coming into view?
A planet, ice-blue and it's winking.

It is begging and beckoning,
Should I? Could I?
Gathering strength, I plummet towards it,
Flying through the sky.

I land in a cold ice cream fountain,
Soaking wet and freezing cold like an iceberg,
Giant marshmallows drag me down, down, down,
Into an abyss with blurry objects to my left and right,
How can I get out? How can I stop? Faster, faster...
Phew! Just my brother pulling me out of bed!

The question is: was it real, was it real?
At first: it can't be, I'm safe here in bed,
Wait... a marshmallow on the desk! What in the world...
'It was not a dream, it was real!' said my head.

Lydia Parry-Balikçi (8)
Springfield Primary School, Sunbury-On-Thames

Space Travel

I'm travelling in my personal red rocket,
Made out of strong chocolate and the seat made from
marshmallows,
My stomach is aching terribly,
Couldn't hold it any longer so off I hopped and...

Once I arrived at the moon,
I was thrilled that it was shaped like a spoon,
The stars were as twinkly as an active magic wand,
This was the most beautiful sight of all my life.

After that I got back in,
Blasted off once again,
But towards Saturn I went,
And met a boy named Kent,
Then he said, 'How are you today?'
I answered back, 'Okay, thank you!'

Next I jumped back in my rocket,
I decided to return back home,
And *whoosh!* the fire blazing behind me,
Then *bang! Crash!* I landed on my roof,
I opened my eyes and I was back in bed.

Shelley Sine Weng (8)
Springfield Primary School, Sunbury-On-Thames

Unicorn Adventure

There was a unicorn called Mr Unicorn
He has rainbow hair
Mr Unicorn shoots out rainbows
He leads people to an unknown land

Mr Unicorn gives sweets to people on the rainbow
He never lets anyone get hurt
Mr Unicorn, you shine at night
He loves adventures
Rainbows follow him everywhere

Suddenly, Mr Unicorn started chasing his tail
When I woke up a horrible sight met my eyes,
Mr Unicorn's horn disappeared
You can't shoot rainbows if you don't have your horn
Out of the clouds his friend came to the rescue
His friend had something for him
It was his rainbow horn

I felt astonished
Mr Unicorn started crying with happiness
Thank you so much
Everyone went to the rainbow and had a party.

Charlotte Hunt (9)
Springfield Primary School, Sunbury-On-Thames

My Minecraft World

My dream started,
I went forward to my dream doors,
To see what dream I would have,
I jumped into my dream door,
My dream is realistic Minecraft World.

I was thrilled with the sight
My feet were warm,
My house I found with a car,
It had a diamond door,
Never quartz for walls and effect,
And stained-glass windows,
Then I found a pig,
The pig on a diamond minecart.

I put a saddle on it,
I got a carrot on a stick,
Then I rode off to the street.
The street was full of candy,
I rode the pig up and high,
Then I went to say goodbye,
I was on the clouds,
Very high,

Then I flew like a bird,
With the pig,
We went to deep space,
It was night so we had to say goodbye.

Harry Dawson (8)
Springfield Primary School, Sunbury-On-Thames

Untitled

I closed my eyes,
Two minutes later I opened them
And I saw a palace named Alice.
I went inside and flew deeper and deeper,
I stopped, a cat appeared.
Suddenly, I gave it some tea,
Shockingly it spoke to me.
Then it began to float,
The cat was in a cage.
He told me his name was Paige,
I felt a bit scared
But I declared I would help the cat.
He found a key but it had wee on it.
Anyway, I picked it up because I had no choice.
I unlocked the cage, the cat ran and gave me a hug.
I surprisingly had wings,
I flew home, my parents were so happy to see me.
My mum said I could keep the cat,
His new name was Mr Fuzzy Pants.

Sherry Ayazi (8)
Springfield Primary School, Sunbury-On-Thames

Dream Come Back

Oh dream, oh dream
Come back, come back
You're better than a book or my favourite colour, black.

In my dream there are stars
They wave at me beautifully
And they're brighter than Mars.

Let me tell you a story
From long, long ago
A dark emperor came to my enchanted forest.

He destroyed everything around him
I had to stop him with my mighty sword
My sword is as strong as a mountain.

With a swish of my sword
He fell down, down, down
Then no one saw him ever again.

That's the story of the dark emperor
And the enchanted forest.

Erika Marulanda (8)
Springfield Primary School, Sunbury-On-Thames

Dream World

Here I am on the clouds,
There can't be one doubt.
I spotted some glittering sand,
I felt my hands within a lovely land.

In my left hand I held a teddy
And in my left eye I saw Freddy.
Freddy was a great old friend of mine,
Which had a great rickety spine.

I suddenly landed on white sand
With drums banging like a band.
I don't know, are people here?
Here I am facing my fear.

My head felt like cold ice,
A draining noise from the pipes.
My eyes flew open and it's just a dream!
Walking and walking I finally found whipped cream!

Jessie Perez Maier (7)
Springfield Primary School, Sunbury-On-Thames

The Game Of Magic

I woke up ready to start another day,
When my sister knocked on the door saying, 'Can we play?'
I said, 'No, I've got to go,'
But she kept begging and begging so I said yes and stayed.
Then I heard the maid and she stayed and played,
She didn't really like the game which was a shame,
But as soon as we were just about to finish the game
We felt weird
And started to think of a beard.
We closed our eyes and listened to the flies in the air
Just when we saw a bear.
We started teleporting in the air
And the maid didn't really care.

Teagan May Leigh Curtis (9)
Springfield Primary School, Sunbury-On-Thames

Harry The Footballer

Once upon a dream there was a man named Harry,
He very much loved his daddy.
He loved football so he wanted to get scouted,
But because he thought he was rubbish he doubted.

His favourite football team was Chelsea,
Soon after in a match he got stung by a bee.
He thought he was as slow as a worm,
'Don't be silly,' said his coach, quite firm.

Eventually he accomplished his dream,
By getting scouted by his favourite football team.
For the achievement he did his celebration dance,
Daze,
So he asked his dad to be his slave.

Leon Elwell (9)
Springfield Primary School, Sunbury-On-Thames

Chocolate Tea

Don't touch me I'm VIP
My pool is filled with chocolate tea
So don't mess with me.

When I listen to someone who is rhyming
I dream of someone bribing
When I frown
I look like a clown
Which may be alright
When I'm bright.

Dogs are my favourite
And they eat my wallet
I go to school
And I play pool
Guess what? I'm very cool.

Do you know who I am yet
Because it's taken you long enough
If I give you a clue, you might just get
I'm filled with sweet chocolatey stuff.

Iona Michelle Ballantyne (11)
Springfield Primary School, Sunbury-On-Thames

My Underwater Kingdom

Little starfish butlers serve me in the sun
While dolphin's splash and play, having tremendous fun
The Sprite- tasting sea makes waves as clear as can be
That can stun anyone
I looked across the majestic palace
Where there was to be no malice
The underwater queen originally from Dallas
Stands with pride and clasps her golden chalice.

The queen eats her lunch
But no animals would she munch
Or humans and fellow mermaids would she punch.

When I woke up with a scream
I was sad to know it was all just a dream!

Rachel Hunt (11)
Springfield Primary School, Sunbury-On-Thames

Elizabeth And The Secret Door

One morning Princess Elizabeth woke up
And started her day.
She rushed downstairs to the dancing room.
Her friends were waiting.
As quick as a flash
She rushed to her bed.
She jumped up
And in a blink of an eye
She saw her grandmother.
She gave her a special book,
She read it all the way to the end of the garden.
Suddenly, she saw a beautiful door covered in flowers.
She opened the door and found herself in Wonderland,
Her dress was as pink as a blossom flower,
She saw magical creatures all around.

Lucy Harrison (8)
Springfield Primary School, Sunbury-On-Thames

World War Three

W e are in danger. The enemy strikes,
O ne million people must fight for our beloved
   country,
R emember the consequences,
L est we forget,
D on't stop fighting.

W e will make our country proud,
A rmed and ready to fight,
R emember to never give up.

T he country is grateful for you,
H urry, your time is running out.
R emember peace is over now,
E nd this war,
E ven if you die, we will never forget you.

Mitchell O'Brien (10)
Springfield Primary School, Sunbury-On-Thames

Dream Land

Everyone is going and no one is slowing,
Dream Land is rising and people are arriving.
The candyfloss are talking and fish are walking,
Everything is fine and dandy,
Until it goes dark and badly.
A menacing grin spreads across the face of danger.
The danger was major,
As shadows are smothered around.
The buildings and castles are covered in rascals
Doing graffiti on their way.
The sparkles and glitter begin to differ,
Should they stay or go away?

Tomasilda Miska (9)
Springfield Primary School, Sunbury-On-Thames

Frightening Frankenstein

In a land far, far away,
a Frankenstein came to play.
The Frankenstein moaned.
The Frankenstein groaned.

He had Frankenstein waiters,
who ate alligators.
In their suits,
they carried their loot.

It's a magical place,
their games are so ace.
It's a dark, mystical dream,
where you will not be seen.

In this place that is not clean,
nothing will gleam.
In the dark of night,
they will not fight.

Louis Lynch (10)
Springfield Primary School, Sunbury-On-Thames

Dinos Vs Dragons

Far away in Mythical Land
There was a massive light
And the light was a fight
Dinos and dragons fighting for the land.

Dinos working together,
Dragons are too,
Armies getting less
And creatures getting injured.

What do they both want?
Why are they doing this?
When will they stop?
I don't know.

Boom! Bash! Everything went flying,
But suddenly everyone stopped,
Then they made a truce.

Mohammed Zainulabadin (9)
Springfield Primary School, Sunbury-On-Thames

Amazing Potions

Potions, potions are everywhere,
Scientists are experimenting,
All I can see are new inventions
And toys coming alive.

I am in a world of wonder,
This is a potion world,
Bubbling gases in jars,
Hot lava in tubes.

My bunny is with me,
She comes alive,
She takes me to space,
We explore planets together.

I feel excited,
A little bit scared,
I think and worry,
We will never come down again!

Rishitha Mamidala (9)
Springfield Primary School, Sunbury-On-Thames

A Dancer Dream

As I walk through the stage door,
I smell hairspray and pride,
I hear tap shoes on the floor
And I see my dream come true.

I slide on my costume,
I do my hair,
I get called on stage,
I see my dream come true.

I feel my heart racing
As the lights dim
And the curtain opens,
I see my dream come true.

I dance, I believe,
I remember my dream,
I look for the audience,
My dream has come true.

Charlotte Seymour (10)
Springfield Primary School, Sunbury-On-Thames

Untitled

Once upon a time
there was a black and blue dragon
guarding a beautiful diamond,
but ninjas with samurai swords came
with their master sensei, Wu.
But the dragon had other dragons breathing fire
and the ninjas had water and dark magic shields.
But the dragons were too powerful and killed the ninjas
but the sensei was still alive,
he killed one of the dragons.
Then the sensei got killed by a dragon,
but they still had the diamond.

Leeyon Phelan (9)
Springfield Primary School, Sunbury-On-Thames

Candy Land

I walked through Candyfloss Land,
I noticed that there were pink candy trees
With sweets growing on the end of the branches,
In the distance there were huge candy rocks smothered
with sugar,
The sky was like heavenly icing.
The grass smelled like Heaven,
Beautiful candy animals came through the candy
bushes,
Skipped to me on the heavenly grass,
There was one thing that everything
Including the guards were made of... candyfloss.

Tegan Denness (9)
Springfield Primary School, Sunbury-On-Thames

Believe You Will Achieve

If you believe you will achieve,
If you don't believe why even try?

You won't achieve your goals if you don't even try,
Just take part and hope your winning counts.

So if you lose don't get in a stress,
There is always next time because...
Your goal is always there for you!

So try your best, work your hardest,
Don't get stressed out if you want to achieve your
dreams!

Zak Bhandari (8)
Springfield Primary School, Sunbury-On-Thames

Fireland

Through Fireland I could see shooting flames out of a
chimney,
As I spotted a crimson house I saw something familiar,
Past the trees and past the bushes, I noticed the leaves
were rustling,
There was a firefox as gorgeous as ever with piercing
black eyes and a bright orange tail,
Stunning animals came from behind bushes dotted
around the forests,
All these animals had one small touch... fire.
These flames made animals beautiful.

Deryn Skye Cotterill (9)
Springfield Primary School, Sunbury-On-Thames

My Nightmare

I'm hiding in a haunted house,
I'm as scared as a mouse,
All around me is black,
All I have to keep warm is my sack.

There are clowns everywhere chasing me,
Should I run? Should I hide
Or should I just be me?

I suddenly see a weird shadow,
What to do? What to do?
I fell into a well that was shallow,
I'm trapped, alone, scared,
Only a minute to live...

Mia Grace Jennings (8)
Springfield Primary School, Sunbury-On-Thames

The Magical Dancer

There once was a dancer
Who had a very nice master.
She practised her ballet all day
But the master wanted to play.
So she took him away,
She said only for today.

While the ballerina was practising
She fell with a thump.
On the floor with a nasty bump,
The master ran her to hospital as quick as lightning.
The doctor said she will be fine,
But the master said she is a dancer.

Amy Wotton (8)
Springfield Primary School, Sunbury-On-Thames

Candy Dream Land

Through the puffs of clouds I could never frown,
I could see a crown,
It was made out of candy,
Everything was fine and dandy.
The Pringle ducks gathered around the sprinkles
While it crinkled.
The ice cream melted through the rice pudding,
People were eating and sleeping,
Their jelly was wobbling in their bellies,
Chocolate, chocolate sprinkles, sprinkles
Everyone was going to have wrinkles.

Michelle Phillips (9)
Springfield Primary School, Sunbury-On-Thames

Unicorn's Magic

The unicorn dazzled in the moonlight that shone from above.
As I watched from a distance, my heart filled with love.

The candyfloss clouds were as fluffy as a pillow,
as they rained Skittles onto a tree which was a willow.

As the unicorns come from above,
you might just see the birds and the doves.

When baby unicorns are born,
a little shimmer shines from their baby horn.

Faye Evans (11)
Springfield Primary School, Sunbury-On-Thames

Cheerleading

C ongratulations for winning

H appiness and smiles

E xcited cheerleaders/gymnasts

E njoying what we do

R epresenting our team

L eading the cheer

E xperiencing your chance

A dream comes true

D ancing in style

I ncredible stunts and tumble

N ever give up

G iving your all.

Tanae Jones-Barnaby (9)

Springfield Primary School, Sunbury-On-Thames

Dreamland

The world is upside down
So now my feet are in the clouds.
Birds can't fly in the sky,
They flap their wings high above.

Above me I see
Swaying trees in the breeze
Too much breeze for the trees
Now they're bouncing all around me.

The clouds below me
Are making me hungry
They look like fluffy cotton candy.

Gracie Denton (9)
Springfield Primary School, Sunbury-On-Thames

Pirates Land!

N othing I can see

I am stranded on a pirate ship

G etting closer to me is a pirate

H e was picking me up

T hrowing me on the plank

'M e plank is a mess!

A s they throw me a net and a brush

R est of my life is living with them

'E scape me ship you can't!' he called to me.

William Weller (8)

Springfield Primary School, Sunbury-On-Thames

Unicorns

U nicorns are beautiful and colourful

N ow unicorns have colourful horns

I am with an extremely cute unicorn

C olourful unicorns are pretty

O nly unicorns have a white mane

R ed unicorns have a lovely red horn

N ow unicorns are all colourful

S ome unicorns have beautiful coloured horns or manes.

Olivia Barlow (7)
Springfield Primary School, Sunbury-On-Thames

The Legend Of Fairies

F airies are my dream world

A nd when I am older I want to be one

I n Pixie Hollow there are thousands of fairies

R ain is the light of fairies

I n Pixie Hollow there are more tinker fairies than any other fairies

E nd of Pixie Hollow is where you will find the main fairy queen

S tay and dream of fairies.

Megan Hewett (8)
Springfield Primary School, Sunbury-On-Thames

Insects

I nsects roam cheerfully in my wonderful kingdom
N o one can trespass here
S piders agree to leave the flies alone
E veryone loves me, so they will miss me
C aterpillars transform into fluttering butterflies
T arantulas are fun to look after
S leeping helps me dream of my paradise.

Morgan Weller (11)
Springfield Primary School, Sunbury-On-Thames

Roller Coaster To Mars

Roller coaster - a great ride,
jump on for great fun.
You have fun that's good.
you're halfway screaming with joy,
until an earthquake strikes.
The track goes away,
away, away it goes.
Into space, half of the Earth goes.
Off we go into space.
You end up permanently on Mars.

Sion Astley (10)
Springfield Primary School, Sunbury-On-Thames

At The Seaside

S easides are my favourite place to be

E ngland is the country I live in

A merica is the place I go on holiday

S now on the seaside

I ride a horse

D o you like the seaside?

E nchanted horse rides in my fluffy bubble in once upon a dream.

Tessy Olliff (8)

Springfield Primary School, Sunbury-On-Thames

Football

F ootball is dramatic

O verhead kicks are fantastic

O ther teams argue with the referee

T ackling may be a little dirty

B icycle kicks are lovely to watch

A nd very exciting to see

L ots of sweating

L ots of injuries.

Jack Garnham (9)
Springfield Primary School, Sunbury-On-Thames

Lonely Dragon

Once there was a dragon
He was lonely, with no one to play with.
But this little boy saw him
And the dragon was in tears.

The little boy went over to him
And said, 'Do you want to play?'
The dragon said yes.
He's now a best friend.

Callum Postins (9)
Springfield Primary School, Sunbury-On-Thames

PS4 Day

P laying PS4 alone in the house
S ucking 20 lollies an hour
4 00,000 cheese balls filling the room.

D ogs keeping me warm and hugging me
A cting like a baboon in a china shop
Y awning like a madman in an office.

Noah Light

Springfield Primary School, Sunbury-On-Thames

I'm A Witch

I am a witch,
A magical witch,
A special witch
Flying on the pitch.

I have a cat,
A magical cat,
A powerful cat
That isn't a brat.

I have a dream,
A very special dream,
A great dream,
I need cream.

Lilia Bouhoune (9)
Springfield Primary School, Sunbury-On-Thames

Football Teams

F ootball is fantastic

O verhead kicks are spectacular

O ver and under we go

T ackling can be dangerous

B all flies over the world

A round the world is amazing

L ots of drama

L ots of injuries.

Kyle Neate (9)
Springfield Primary School, Sunbury-On-Thames

Money Sky

Money falling from the sky,
Come back, please don't fly,
You will make my heart break,
Come back please and don't be fake,
I will sing a song to you about when you were being fake,
But you managed to change for your own sake.

Albanie Barrett (9)
Springfield Primary School, Sunbury-On-Thames

The Escape Of The Star Island 2

I was on an island
But the island was destroyed.
Then I saw another island,
It was shiny like the stars.
I made a cave for myself
And for the footballers too.
Then I had a great idea,
The footballers would be my army.

Alan Jakub Kraczewski (7)
Springfield Primary School, Sunbury-On-Thames

The Station Attack

T he midnight hour came
R eady to go and play with my play friends
A strange light appeared
I was terrified
N ow I was running away from a witch while carrying my dog!

Elodie Jeans Trouabal-Weremczuk (8)
Springfield Primary School, Sunbury-On-Thames

The Dragon

Once there was a wizard
Sitting in the forest,
Caught in a bush all alone.
Thud! went the dragon.
Smack! went the tree
And down fell the wizard for his tea.

Jacob Ieuan Davies (8)
Springfield Primary School, Sunbury-On-Thames

The Best Dancer

I'm going to see a dance
With my fabulous teacher.
It's going to be fabulous,
It's going to be amazing.

Abigail Garen Larsen (7)
Springfield Primary School, Sunbury-On-Thames

The Joyful Dream

I fell into a deep sleep,
Something extremely weird was about to happen.
It was so unusual; then all of a sudden, *boom!*
I saw something right before my eyes.
The purple moor with stars,
Twinkling and glistening in the sky.
It was a flame coming out of a jar,
It was violet, burgundy and pink.
I fell into another dimension.
I could see myself in all of the mirrors surrounding me.
I put my hand through one of them.
I was so intrigued to find out
I time-travelled to the future.
I saw my future self,
I also got a Grammy award.
I looked in this history book and I could see myself.
I was so proud, I'm always remembered by the public.
I woke up with tears of joy,
Celebrating in the kitchen,
Eating my favourite chocolate cake.

Zaria Hinds (10)
St Cyprian's Greek Orthodox Primary Academy, Thornton Heath

The Pet Store

mine

In a pet store I looked around,
I saw the pets, who were really rather loud.
In the place it was a disgrace.
People, you'll see scary animals in your face.

It was very weird being around stuff hairy,
Also you must trust me, the cats are really scary.
One of the cats had hard scratches,
It is almost like you were hurt by matches.

This cat wanted to hurt me all the time,
I would really rather eat disgusting lime.
We all wanted to find out why,
I really think I needed to fix my eye.

Suddenly the cat turned all fat,
Then he sat on a muddy mat.
It was so frightening,
Just like a big flash of lightning.

I woke up and saw my nice pet mouse,
Then I knew that I was safe in my house.

Lamek Samson (7)
St Cyprian's Greek Orthodox Primary Academy, Thornton Heath

best poem of all.

83

My Secret Garden

My secret garden
Is full of wonderful secrets
I can tell you them
If only you lock and seal it.

It has the rarest flowers in the world
Kept in a special place
There is a posh restaurant there
Full of all my favourite foods.

My secret garden
Is an endless heaven
I discovered it when I was seven
It is a beautiful paradise.

Loads of creatures live there too
Butterflies, ladybugs, cats and rabbits
Honestly, it's like a real zoo!
I love it here.

In my secret garden
Flower fairies roam
And look after the flowers
When I go home.

I can make my own flowers
I never share the recipes
They are my prized possessions
And close to me.

Deon Nunoo (11)
St Cyprian's Greek Orthodox Primary Academy, Thornton Heath

My Dream Land

One day, when the Earth was upside down
I was looking outside my window.
My house was made out of gingerbread,
Windows warheads, chimney toxic waste
And a pool full of jelly.
And finally the bedroom and kitchen gummies.
I was once walking outside with my cousins
And all of a sudden the earth shook.
I thought I was going to fall as hard as toffee.
I didn't, but I did shake.
After that, when I shook my hand
A wrist band appeared.
There was a unicorn on it and it dropped off.
The pink wrist band then created a real-life unicorn.
I got on the unicorn's back
And we went to Candy Land.
It was so tasty and so fun.
I had a great time with my new pet unicorn.

Isabelle Bradbury (9)
St Cyprian's Greek Orthodox Primary Academy, Thornton Heath

The Big Match

In a friendly house seven not eleven kids creep in
So they could be sleeping in a bed like a ted.
Lenny opened the door to a cupboard,
Inside a ball like a bowl.

It pulled them in with a whoosh!
And when it sucked them in.
They found themselves on a giant pitch.
The match started, they felt like bark,
Then went spark and got off to a good start.

Then they scored, they all went cluck
And then bark! It was half-time.
They went zing and bing and ding!
In the changing room of doom!

In the next half they went barf!
The last shot got lost in the moss.
The ball got lost, the boss got cross.

Daniel Cort (8)
St Cyprian's Greek Orthodox Primary Academy, Thornton Heath

I Had A Dream

I had a dream that I could fly,
Next thing I knew I was up in the sky.
I had a dream I was a pirate,
All of a sudden I became a pilot.
I had a dream that I lived on the sun,
Accidentally I burnt my bum!
I had a dream that I was a bird
But still I was a nerd.
I had a dream that I was in a Lamborghini,
I felt so cool but nobody could see me.
I had a dream that I became a nurse
But then I went shopping for a new purse.
I had a dream I met Donald Trump,
I accidentally kicked him on his leg,
He had a big bump.
I had a dream I went to China
Then I also travelled to the famous Asia Minor.

Nastasia Tingle (11)
St Cyprian's Greek Orthodox Primary Academy, Thornton Heath

Frightful Wish

Oh look, a shooting star!
I've always wanted magic powers
But I do feel sorry for our old car.
I've smelt so many flowers...

But I prefer powers.
I wish for them and I am in another land.
Full of wonder and colourful fish.
I look at the yellow sand.

But it is a big, friendly dragon!
He was carrying a wagon!
I set him free today
As we both flee away.

We met some fairies and a unicorn
That had a sharp, pointy horn!
We were enemies of a monster
That turned into a lobster.

But then we defeated him
And I went back to my land.

Ellie Todorova (7)
St Cyprian's Greek Orthodox Primary Academy, Thornton Heath

A Happy Place

I was in a very happy place last night,
And nobody could find it
Cos it's in a hiding place!

I was looking for my doll under my bed
And I saw a door on the floor,
Waiting for me to get in!

There was a secret garden,
Like the most spectacular place,
With a lot of grass and trees
And a little house
Which was made from chocolate
And colourful flowers.

I woke up my friend quickly,
I led them to the door,
To play every single time
In the most beautiful place!

Ioanna Karanasiou (9)
St Cyprian's Greek Orthodox Primary Academy, Thornton Heath

Nightmares' Blood

N ights get scary

I magination turns to fire

G oblins whisper in your ear

H airy wolves suck your blood

T eachers turn to clowns

M ums scream, 'Argh!' and die

A nimals turn to stone

R acers stop driving

E lephants stomp on you

S cars stick in your head

B lood drips out of your ear

L oving sisters go to skeleton and ash

O n, on and on

O ut you go

D on't go to sleep!

Peggy Stack (8)
St Cyprian's Greek Orthodox Primary Academy, Thornton Heath

Santa Claus

Santa Claus is a boss
On his sleigh with staff that look like a horse
His house, covered in snow
Santa's house is really far around the north
Has minions called elves
Stacking on top of each other to get to shelves
Giving toys to goody-goodies
Gets toys like Woody in a hoody

S anta is full of banter
A nd he is really cool
N ot being naughty will prove you're not a fool
T he awesome guy
A s he is really up high.

Tyler Price-Frankson (11)
St Cyprian's Greek Orthodox Primary Academy, Thornton Heath

The Dinosaur And Dragon World

N ight-time came and there was a little wizard

I was very scared and a

G reat big thunder came and took me to Dragon Land

H e was really evil and we saw a dinosaur, a

T -rex was chasing us everywhere

M y mummy was screaming, everyone was screaming

A nd we hid in a bush. The bush was magical and we

R an back home quickly. The wizard was gone

E very day we were very happy

S o that is the end of the scary poem.

Alyssa Ama Amponsah (8)

St Cyprian's Greek Orthodox Primary Academy, Thornton Heath

Nightmare!

I start sweating all over.
I know when I close my eyes
I will fall into a deep nightmare.
I breathe in and then out.
I close my eyes and then fall into a dark land.
Clowns, vampires, zombies
And other scary creatures surround me.
I look around but there is nowhere to go.
The creatures start coming towards me.
I knew that this was the end of me.
Then suddenly a light as bright
As the sun swept over me.
When it faded away
I was safe in my comfy bed.

Yolanda-Jewel Michael (8)
St Cyprian's Greek Orthodox Primary Academy, Thornton Heath

Unicorns!

Unicorns, unicorns
Under an sparkling apple tree
Is this true?
This is definitely not true!

Walking down the field
I bumped into a candy house
I ate some candy, it was really amazing.

Under the tree the unicorns get hurt
It is magic, they all are hurt
'Oh no, I can't help all of you.'

The butterflies are lovely
In the field
I am so surprised and happy.

Shayla-Skye Salmon (7)
St Cyprian's Greek Orthodox Primary Academy, Thornton Heath

Candy World Adventure

Once upon a dream I wish...
In my dreams I was imagining Candy Land.
Then it came true, *bang!*
The candy was as yum as popcorn.

Then me and my friends sat on a mat with a cat.
The cat said, 'Do you love candy?
It looks like Mandy.'
'Who's Mandy?' I asked with my friends.
'Mandy is my cat friend.'
We took that cat home.
I went home and lived happily ever after.

Zemira Hinds (7)
St Cyprian's Greek Orthodox Primary Academy, Thornton Heath

A Nightmare

One eye closes so does the other,
I snuggle under my cover.
I put my head back on the pillow
As everything turns dark and hollow.
A spider comes out,
A clown too.
'I don't like this!'
As I hear a hiss,
It's a snake.
'Stop, stop!'
'I want this to stop!'
I wake up so terrified,
But to my surprise,
It was just a nightmare,
A dark, spooky nightmare.

Alex Todorov (11)
St Cyprian's Greek Orthodox Primary Academy, Thornton Heath

Helping The Lion Find His Family

When I was a young, smart girl
I went to a jungle to study lions.
It was really hot in this jungle.
Suddenly I saw a lost baby lion dying on the ground
So I immediately ran to the baby lion
And carried it in my warm arms.
I didn't want to leave it there
In this dangerous jungle
So I helped it to look for its family.
Then I heard a roar
So I followed the roar and found his family.

Shanai Thomas (8)
St Cyprian's Greek Orthodox Primary Academy, Thornton Heath

I'm Famous

I hear the laughter of children
I hear the applause and cheers
As I close my eyes tightly
Hanging over the platform
Holding my breath
Hoping to dive into the water.

1, 2, 3, *splash!*
I dive in the water with a smirk
I dive so deep just to realise that it's a dream.

Maybe one day I'll become a famous diver...
Some day.

Teairra Blissett (11)
St Cyprian's Greek Orthodox Primary Academy, Thornton Heath

Footballer

I can see
A footballer gazing
Like I'm going to be a footballer.

I'm in Hollywood
In a football stadium.

This is what happened...
I walked into the stadium.

I'm with the football player, Ronaldo.
I feel like a wrecking ball
Because I'm so pumped.

I watch the player, Ronaldo play,
He is so cool!

Shamai Holder (8)
St Cyprian's Greek Orthodox Primary Academy, Thornton Heath

Dragons

D readful dragons joking around and loud

R oaring so loud some faint with a storm cloud

A ll the dragons scare me and I run away

'G ot to stay out of sight,' I say so that I'm OK.

'O h no,' says I, 'a dragon has come for me!'

'N o, no, no!' I'm trapped but now I can see.

S o it's just a nightmare.

Alana Shabazz (7)

St Cyprian's Greek Orthodox Primary Academy, Thornton Heath

My Family!

F amily are the best thing I have ever had.

A mazing and wonderful, I have the cutest sisters in the world, they care for me and love me.

M y mum and dad care for me.

I have a very wonderful family who love me.

L iving with my family is amazing. I love them with all my heart.

Y ou and I have an amazing journey to spend our lives together.

Crystal-Anne Michael (10)
St Cyprian's Greek Orthodox Primary Academy, Thornton Heath

Concert Dream Of Fear

I'm as scared as can be
No one is with me
There are people watching
I'm on stage, I can't breathe.

The concert is as scary as a bee
I get stage fright
And it frightens me
I jump and I can fly.

As I come out everyone throws food towards me
I also scream and I sleep walk like a tree
I wake up and see it was a dream.

Avaie Henry (8)
St Cyprian's Greek Orthodox Primary Academy, Thornton Heath

Lost In Caramel World

When I come into Candy World
I see the whitest alicorn
With the pretty unicorn.
I'm with my nice grandma
And my cute as a candy cat called Sniffles.
Candy World is located in Mertropolis.
We feel hungry, excited and enthusiastic.
Even Sniffles.
We find a mysterious place called Caramel World.
The place had caramel.
We live there happily.

Glynise Kobiah (8)
St Cyprian's Greek Orthodox Primary Academy, Thornton Heath

Nightmare!

N obody knew she was dancing,

I n the cupboard a spider was prancing.

G et out! Creepy creature that's pink,

H ave you seen it do that scary wink?

T urn around for a fright,

M ummy, you're so right!

A re you gonna leave

R olling down a tree?

E veryone was scared, even though it was a dream!

Megan Findlator (8)

St Cyprian's Greek Orthodox Primary Academy, Thornton Heath

Superpowers!

It was dark,
Nobody saw me,
But then the clock fell down,
I was worried and went to bed,
When I woke up I was sad.
Then suddenly I lit up,
I was happy not sad.
People saw me glowing in the dark,
Then suddenly I had powers.
Many people saw the dark
And said, 'Is it bad?'
But then I said, 'Boo!'
They were scared!

Alicia Okonma (9)
St Cyprian's Greek Orthodox Primary Academy, Thornton Heath

My Powers

My powers are strong and save the day.
My powers are cool and are fun to play.

They rescue young, they rescue old
But my secret will never be told.

I flash past like a lightning bolt
But when someone is in need, the fun comes to a halt.

I'll never lose, I am a saviour.
You'll go to jail for bad behaviour.

Tiana Paige Tal (11)
St Cyprian's Greek Orthodox Primary Academy, Thornton Heath

Beautiful Fairies

Fairies, fairies in my dream,
Fairies, fairies, ones called Mary,
I go to a kingdom with my aunty,
A lovely party at the kingdom.

I meet a fairy at the party,
I draw a picture that's so arty,
I drink some punch with my lunch.

We become fairies,
We have crowns,
Goodbye fairy,
We had a nice time!

Fega Omoma (8)
St Cyprian's Greek Orthodox Primary Academy, Thornton Heath

My Unicorn

M y eyes close themselves
Y awning, I fade into my dream

U nicorns run around me
N o other unicorn is the same as mine
I jump onto your silky back
C lip-clop your rainbow hooves go
O n and on you gallop
R iding in the sweet-scented clouds
N ow I will sleep tight.

Ana-Maria Cornea (11)
St Cyprian's Greek Orthodox Primary Academy, Thornton Heath

My Baby Sister

My baby sister is as nice as the smell of perfume.
My baby sister is cleverer than a cheeky monkey.
My baby sister is cuter than a newborn baby.
My baby sister is sometimes more annoying
than an annoying cat.
My baby sister is as caring
as a poor old woman.
I love my baby sister
and she loves me too.

Blessing Babalola (9)
St Cyprian's Greek Orthodox Primary Academy, Thornton Heath

Fairyland Blast!

Fairyland blast is very fast
It might not even be able to last
Oh my, oh dear, we cannot fear
The music is good to hear
And the baby is crying with tears
Flowers here, flowers there
Flowers are everywhere
It's time, it's time for cotton candy
It might even come in handy.

Rihanna Malcolm-Moore (8)
St Cyprian's Greek Orthodox Primary Academy, Thornton Heath

Dark Skies

I looked down at the pitch-black floor
To see no more.
As the dark skies surround me
I see a black figure in the distance
To figure my resistance.
The floor drops down as do I.
All I know is there's nothing more to do.
I then fade away into the real world
As I wake up.

Photios Yiannaki (11)
St Cyprian's Greek Orthodox Primary Academy, Thornton Heath

Weirdness

There are spiders everywhere.
They don't have lots of hair.
I turn into a frog.
The floor turns into a bog.
I fall in.
I realise I have a fin.

I can fly.
I fear I have to die.
Before I say bye-bye
I have to cry.

Jaydon Wesley (7)
St Cyprian's Greek Orthodox Primary Academy, Thornton Heath

Funland

F un is the key
U ndo your dreams and go into them
N othing can stop me
L and of joy
A nd you're the creator
N o wonder you don't want to be here
D o whatever you want.

Eli Julian Joseph Zoil (9)
St Cyprian's Greek Orthodox Primary Academy, Thornton Heath

Running Down The Street

I saw a volcano which shoots out candy
And a chocolate lake and house
Made out of candy canes and marshmallows
I saw candyfloss falling from the sky
And when it rained it rained strawberry milkshake.

Sienna Ellul (9)
St Cyprian's Greek Orthodox Primary Academy, Thornton Heath

Lights Out

Suddenly a figure pops out
Her name is Diana
All of the lights go out
And it is pitch-black
Lights go back on
She appears in your face
Diana eats you
And drinks your blood
You are gone!

Mohammad Zakaria (11)
St Cyprian's Greek Orthodox Primary Academy, Thornton Heath

Loving Pet

You're beautiful, you're cute and loving
You're furry, you're joyful, you're happy
You're everything I have always wanted
Now go to sleep
Your fantastic dreams await.

Artemis Apostolopoulou (11)
St Cyprian's Greek Orthodox Primary Academy, Thornton Heath

Untitled

Running up a hill with hearts coming out of it.
Sky is as blue as the sea.
Clouds raining hearts.
Birds fly in the blue sky.
Cupcakes on trees.
How lovely it can be.

Natalia Phillipou (9)
St Cyprian's Greek Orthodox Primary Academy, Thornton Heath

Me And My BFF In A Haunted House

Spooky, squeaking door,
I'm trapped.
I can't find my way out.
Spiders were everywhere.
Thunder claps.
I run and run.
I hide in the cupboard.

Nathan Gonzalez Gabino (9)
St Cyprian's Greek Orthodox Primary Academy, Thornton Heath

My Poem

There was lots of snow falling very softly
Everywhere on trees, smiling
Snow was fun but disappeared
It came back again but melted.
Sad.

Kwabena Boakye (8)
St Cyprian's Greek Orthodox Primary Academy, Thornton Heath

Bed Poem

Why do I sleep in this filthy bed?
I will live if I stay in this bed.
No I will not, not, not stay in this pongy bed.
The stairs outside my bedroom go
Creak, creak, creak! like a door swinging open.
The planks on my bed go *spring, spring, spring!*
Like the strongest man in the world
Is jumping on a trampoline.

Midnight strikes, the witching hour has started.
Mums and dads are asleep.
Something's in my bedroom.
It's near my bed!
It's only me!

Mina Janes (8)
St Martin's CE (A) Junior School, Epsom

Every Night

Every night I get the fright,
Like it's just a dream.
Every night I get the fright,
Of the clown that's scaring me.
Every night I get the fright,
That the clowns are coming after me.
Every night I get the fright,
Of me hearing spirits scream.

Tasneem Islam (7)
St Martin's CE (A) Junior School, Epsom

Candyland

Candyfloss everywhere
Lollipops in my hair
All sticky and all sweet
Cups of chocolate I eat
The sun is dancing all the way down
It's time to go
All the way in the candyfloss snow
I feel a bit sad
But I know it's time to go.

Elaine Woodward (8)
St Martin's CE (A) Junior School, Epsom

 Young**Writers**
Est.1991

YOUNG WRITERS INFORMATION

We hope you have enjoyed reading this book – and
that you will continue to in the coming years.

If you're a young writer who enjoys reading and creative writing,
or the parent of an enthusiastic poet or story writer,
do visit our website **www.youngwriters.co.uk**. Here you will
find free competitions, workshops and games, as well as
recommended reads, a poetry glossary and our blog.

If you would like to order further copies of this book,
or any of our other titles, then please give us a
call or visit **www.youngwriters.co.uk**.

Young Writers
Remus House
Coltsfoot Drive
Peterborough
PE2 9BF
(01733) 890066
info@youngwriters.co.uk